STAR
PATIENT

© SmileMakers | #MEDI

Facts About

Space

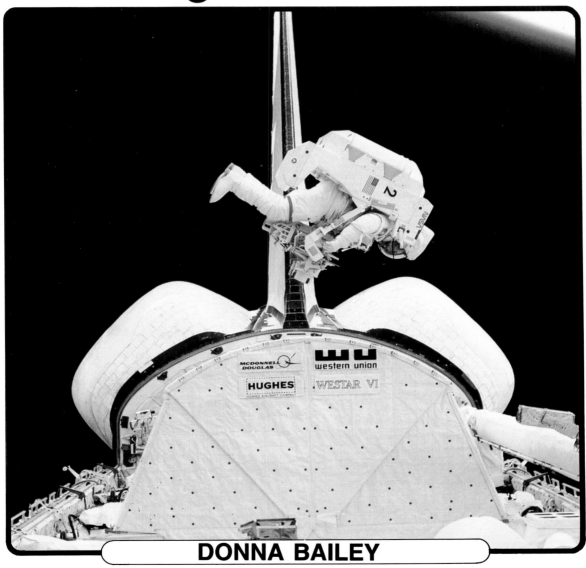

DONNA BAILEY

STECK-VAUGHN
L I B R A R Y
Austin, Texas

How to Use This Book

This book tells you many things about space. There is a Table of Contents on the next page. It shows you what each double page of the book is about. For example, pages 32 and 33 tell you about ''Space Stations.''

On most of these pages you will find words that are printed in **bold** type. The bold type shows you that these words are in the glossary on pages 46 and 47. The glossary explains the meaning of some words that may be new to you.

At the very end of the book there is an index. The index tells you where to find certain words in the book. For example, you can use the index to look up words like probe, astronaut, gravity, and many other words to do with space.

Published in the United States in 1990 by Steck-Vaughn Co., Austin, Texas, a subsidiary of National Education Corporation.

© Macmillan Children's Books 1988
Artwork © BLA Publishing Limited 1988

Material used in this book first appeared in Macmillan World Library: *Space travel.* Published by Macmillan Children's Books

Designed by Julian Holland

Printed and bound in the United States

1 2 3 4 5 6 7 8 9 0 LB 94 93 92 91 90

Library of Congress Cataloging-in-Publication Data

Bailey, Donna.
    Space

    (Facts about)
    Summary: Text and pictures present a basic introduction to space exploration, from rockets to men on the moon to space stations.
    1. Astronautics—Juvenile literature.
[1. Astronautics.   2. Outer space—Exploration]
I. Title.   II. Series: Facts about (Austin, Tex.)
TL793.B22   1990   629.4   89-21762
ISBN 0-8114-2504-5

Contents

Introduction

For hundreds of years people looked at the Moon and stars through **telescopes** and wondered about exploring space.

On October 4, 1956, the Soviet Union launched the first space **satellite**. Since then people have explored the **surface** of the Moon, and in 1987 a Soviet **astronaut** lived in a space station for nearly a year without returning to Earth.

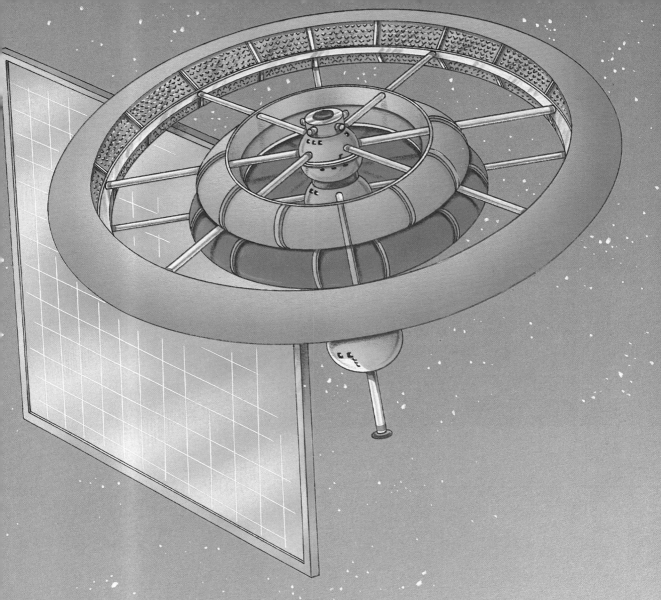

In the future people may live and
work on huge space stations.
These might look like huge wheels.
People would live inside a ''tire''
around the rim of the space station.
Solar panels would get power from
the Sun to make electricity.

The Earth and Space

Earth is surrounded by a layer of air that we breathe. The air gets thinner the higher we go.

When you throw a ball into the air, it
comes down some distance away
from you because of the pull of **gravity**.
If you throw it harder, the ball goes
higher and lands farther away.
If you could throw the ball at 25,000 mph
it would escape the pull of gravity
and go into space. Spacecraft
need the power from **rockets**
to escape from the Earth's gravity.

**gravity pulls the ball
to the ground**

Rockets

This giant Saturn 5 rocket is 365 feet high. The Apollo spacecraft on top of it was only about ten feet high.

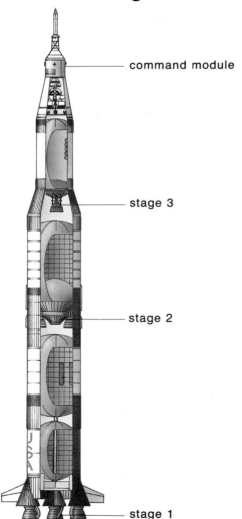

command module

stage 3

stage 2

stage 1

When a spacecraft is launched, the first stage rocket burns fiercely for two and a half minutes to lift the spacecraft into the air.

The burned out rocket separates from the spacecraft and falls back to Earth. The second stage rocket fires to make the spacecraft go faster. When it burns out and falls back to Earth, the third stage rocket fires to take the spacecraft to the Moon.

how a spacecraft lands

A spacecraft travels very fast and gets very hot, so a **heat shield** stops it from burning up.

A **parachute** opens to slow the spacecraft down so it can splash safely into the sea.

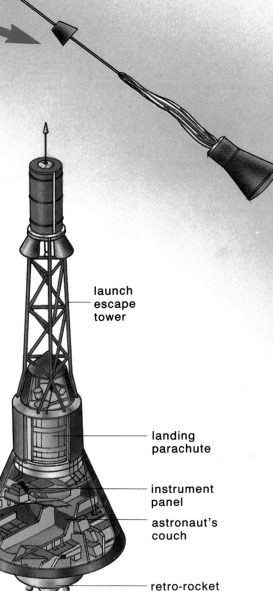

launch escape tower

landing parachute

instrument panel

astronaut's couch

retro-rocket

the Mercury spacecraft

Astronauts in Space

Both the United States and the Soviet Union soon began to send spacecraft with more than one person on board into orbit. When a spacecraft is in orbit, things will float around if they are not fastened down. If you hold a cup and then let it go, it will not fall. This is called **weightlessness**. Our picture shows astronaut Edward Gibson during a space flight.

He seems to be able to lift with only one finger a weightless fellow astronaut.

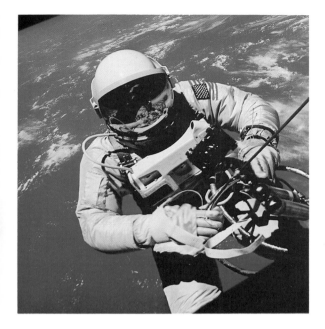

Ed White was the first American to walk in space. He wore an **oxygen pack** on his chest for breathing and was linked to the spacecraft by a 26 foot lifeline. He held a small space gun that fired a **jet** of gas, to move around.

Ed White floats in space

he fires a space gun to move

The Moon

Our picture shows a close-up view of the Moon taken from the Apollo 11 spacecraft on its way back to Earth.

The dark patches on the Moon are called "seas."

There are also tall mountain ranges and hundreds of circular markings called **craters** that cover the Moon's surface. The surface of the Moon is covered with a thin layer of dust. The Moon has no air and no water, so nothing lives or grows there. The Moon also has less gravity than the Earth.

Our picture shows that a girl on the Moon would be able to jump six times higher than she could on the Earth.

a large Moon crater

you can jump much higher on the Moon

Closer to the Moon

Before the Americans could land people on the Moon, they needed photographs to find a good landing site. They sent up **unmanned** Ranger **probes** to take close-up views of the Moon's surface.

The next step was to put some probes into orbit around the Moon.

Our picture shows how probes called Lunar Orbiters were launched from the Earth to circle the Moon.

They went around the Moon several thousand times taking many photographs.

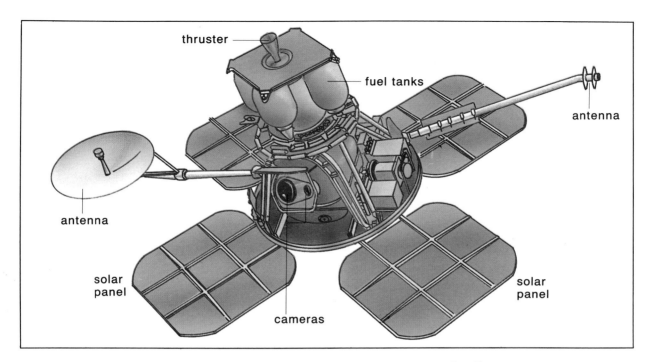

thruster

fuel tanks

antenna

antenna

solar panel

solar panel

cameras

The Lunar Orbiter carried two cameras that were powered by solar panels. One was used for close-up shots, the other for views. The pictures were sent by radio signals to Earth.

This is a photograph of the far side of the Moon taken by the Orbiter.

a Lunar Orbiter

the far side of the Moon

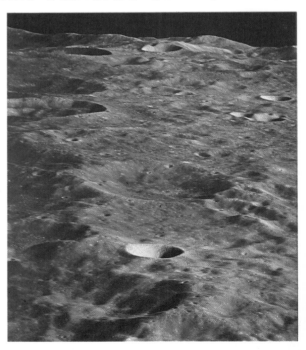

17

Robots on the Moon

In February 1966 the Soviet space probe Luna 9 was the first probe to land on the Moon, and send back TV pictures of the Moon's surface.

Luna 16 brought back soil **samples** to Earth in September 1970.

The Lunokhod Moonwalker in our picture was the first moving **robot** on the Moon. It was controlled by a team on Earth and could climb slopes and weave in and out of craters.

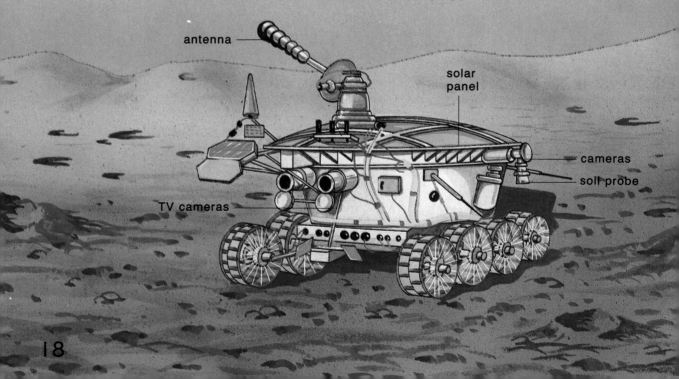

antenna

solar panel

cameras

soil probe

TV cameras

The American probes
to the Moon could not
move around, but they
scooped up samples of
lunar soil, and sent
thousands of pictures
back to Earth.

These showed that a
manned Moon landing
was possible.

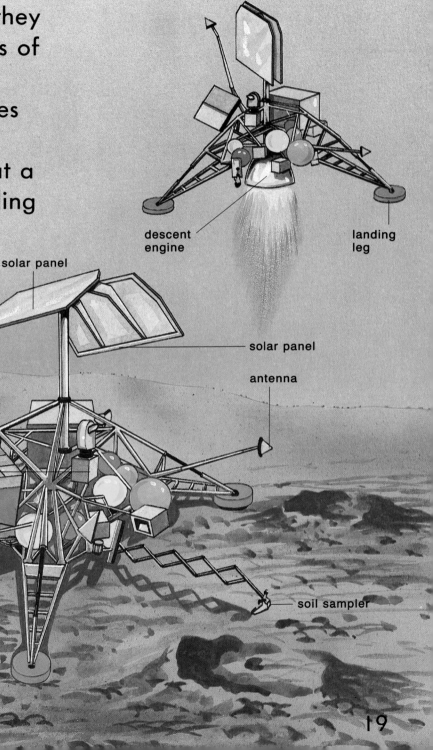

descent
engine

landing
leg

solar panel

solar panel

antenna

antenna

TV camera

soil sampler

Living in Space

In space there is no air to breathe,
no food to eat, and no water to drink.

A spacecraft has **life-support
systems**, so the astronauts do not
have to wear space suits inside.

Our picture shows astronaut Owen
Garriott at work inside Skylab.

Outside the space station, the astronauts wear space suits and carry small life-support systems on their back-packs. They use a manned maneuvering unit like a chair that squirts jets of gas to move around.

Mission Control

Our picture shows Apollo 13 and its Saturn 5 rocket on the launch platform. The huge caterpillar tractor is taking the rocket to the launch site.

The launch of the rocket is checked at the Launch Control Center (LCC) and the controller gives the **countdown** to **lift-off**.

After lift-off, the LCC hands over to the flight controllers at Mission Control Center (MCC).

During the flight, the spacecraft is checked the whole time by computers at the MCC that ''talk'' to the computers on the spacecraft.

the launch of Apollo 11

Mission Control Center

An Apollo Mission

CM	**Command Module** Control center and living quarters
SM	**Service Module** Contains main rocket engine
CSM	**Command and Service Module** Command Module plus Service Module
LM	**Lunar Module** For descent onto and ascent from moon
SLMA	**Spacecraft Lunar Module Adaptor** Links Apollo spacecraft to rocket

Our pictures show how an Apollo spacecraft is launched from the Earth, lands on the Moon, and then returns to the Earth.

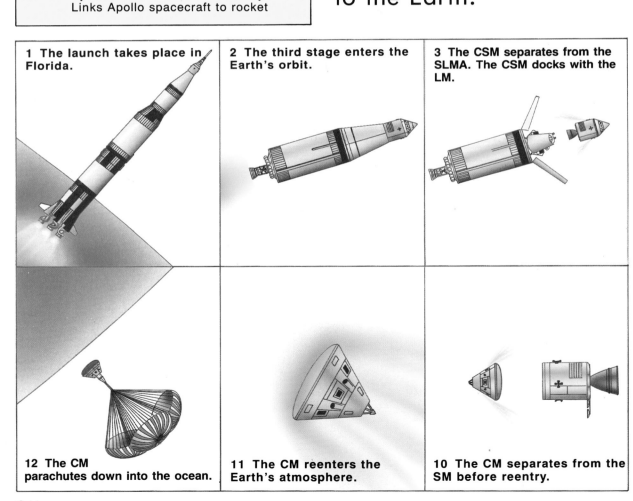

1 The launch takes place in Florida.

2 The third stage enters the Earth's orbit.

3 The CSM separates from the SLMA. The CSM docks with the LM.

12 The CM parachutes down into the ocean.

11 The CM reenters the Earth's atmosphere.

10 The CM separates from the SM before reentry.

The command module is the control center of the spacecraft. The crew sits inside it when the spacecraft is launched from Earth and when it returns to Earth. The lunar module is used to land on the Moon, so the astronauts enter it from the command module just when they are ready to land on the Moon. Then the lunar module separates from the command module.

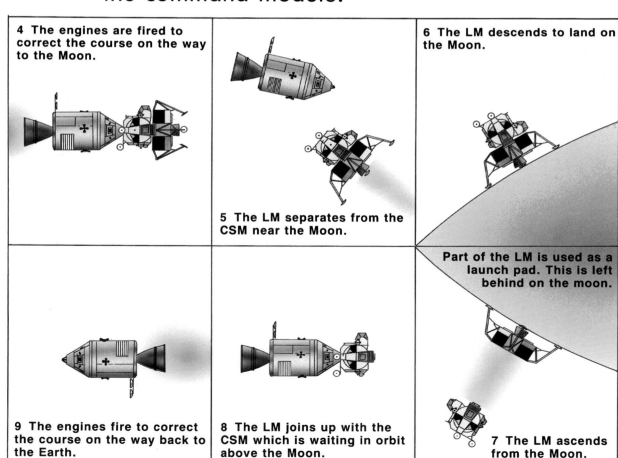

4 The engines are fired to correct the course on the way to the Moon.

5 The LM separates from the CSM near the Moon.

6 The LM descends to land on the Moon.

Part of the LM is used as a launch pad. This is left behind on the moon.

9 The engines fire to correct the course on the way back to the Earth.

8 The LM joins up with the CSM which is waiting in orbit above the Moon.

7 The LM ascends from the Moon.

Men on the Moon

Our photographs show the mission of Apollo 11 in 1969, when two Americans were the first people to set foot on the Moon.

The command module orbited the Moon while Neil Armstrong and Edwin Aldrin crawled into the lunar module. This came down to land on a flat area clear of rocks on the Moon.

The astronauts put on their space suits. On July 21, 1969, Neil Armstrong was the first human to set foot on the Moon.

the lunar module on the way to the Moon

the first step

Armstrong and Aldrin took photographs, set up scientific experiments, and collected rocks. They returned to the lunar module and blasted off from the Moon.

They **docked** with the command module. Aldrin and Armstrong crawled back into the command module that splashed down safely on July 24 in the Pacific Ocean.

Aldrin setting up an experiment

men open the command module in the ocean

The Apollo Spacecraft

Our picture shows the three parts of the Apollo spacecraft. The crew sat in the command module for launch and landing. The service module carried the engines, air, and water supplies. The lunar module landed on the Moon.

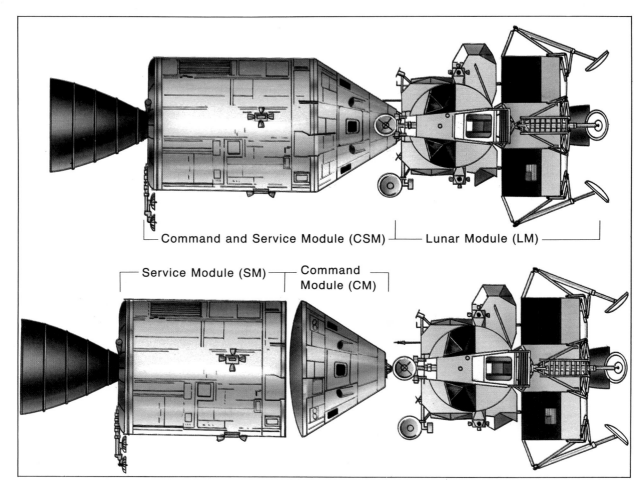

Command and Service Module (CSM) — Lunar Module (LM)

Service Module (SM) — Command Module (CM)

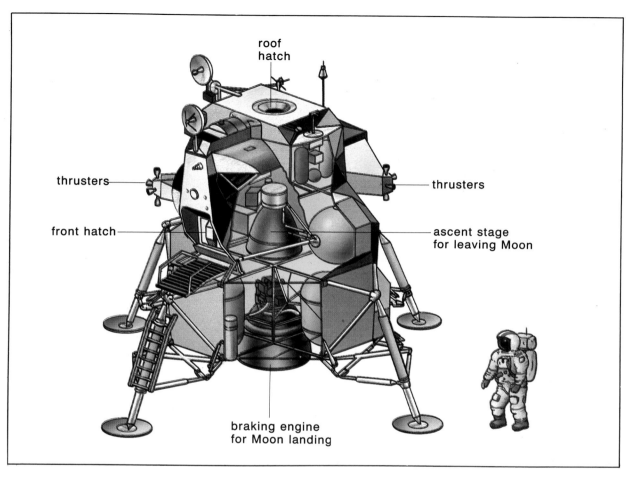

roof
hatch

thrusters

thrusters

front hatch

ascent stage
for leaving Moon

braking engine
for Moon landing

The lunar module was 23 feet high
when its four legs were extended.
It had a roof **hatch** for docking with
the command module, as well as a
front hatch to let the astronauts get out
onto the surface of the Moon.

The bottom half of the module was
used as a launch pad and was left on
the Moon when the astronauts made
their ascent to the command module.

29

The Lunar Rover

Apollo 15 was the first mission to carry the Lunar Roving Vehicle, a car with a top speed of 10.5 miles per hour.

You can see the tracks of the astronauts and the Lunar Rover in the lunar dust. The lunar module is in the background.

The Lunar Rover could carry two crew members and equipment. It was used on three missions to explore the Moon's surface up to 22 miles from the spacecraft. The crews collected rocks and samples of lunar soil.

The **antenna** shaped like an umbrella sent **radio signals** back to the Earth.

Our pictures show the Lunar Rover on the Moon, and Dr. Jack Schmitt standing near a huge rock, on the final Moon mission.

31

Space Stations

The first space station, Salyut 1, was built by the Soviets in 1971. The Americans launched a space station called Skylab in 1973.

Our picture shows how an Apollo spacecraft docked with Skylab.

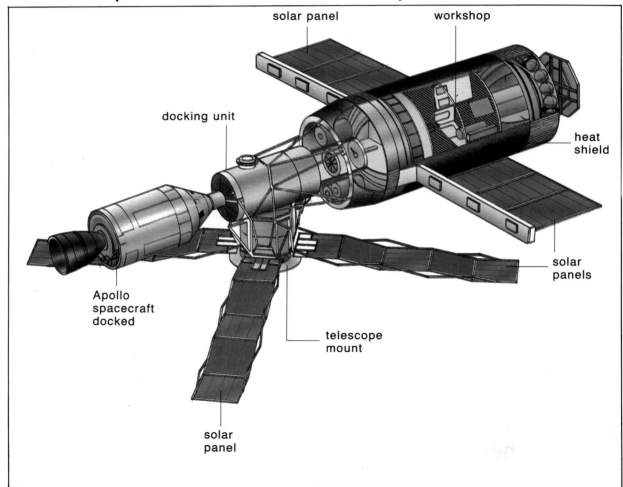

solar panel

workshop

docking unit

heat shield

solar panels

Apollo spacecraft docked

telescope mount

solar panel

There were several problems during the launch of Skylab. The heat shield was damaged and one of the solar panels was torn off.

The first Skylab crew repaired the remaining solar panel, and put a yellow "sunshade" on the side to keep the space station cool.

Skylab after repairs had been carried out

Inside Skylab the crews worked on various scientific experiments.

Our picture shows two Skylab crewmen inside the workshop. Their feet are strapped to the floor to stop them from floating around.

inside Skylab

33

Probes into Space

Scientists use probes to explore other planets.

In 1976 scientists sent a robot probe, Viking 2, to land on Mars. The photographs it took showed that the surface of Mars was a red stony desert with no signs of life.

In 1981 Voyager passed close to the giant planet Saturn on its way to Uranus. Then it flew on to the more distant planet Neptune in 1989.

Robot probes have also been sent to look at **comets**.

Our artist's picture shows the Giotto probe passing through Halley's comet.

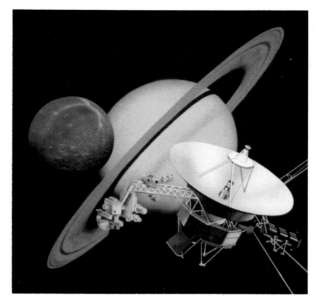

Voyager 2 passing by one of Neptune's ten moons

the Giotto probe

The Space Shuttle

The Space Shuttle was the first real spaceship that could go into orbit around Earth and land on a runway on its return.

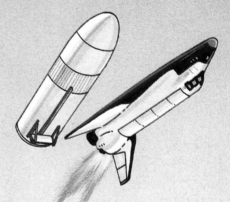

Our picture shows how the Space Shuttle separates from **rocket boosters** and the fuel tank after takeoff.

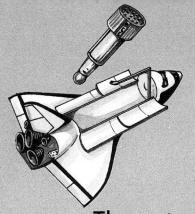
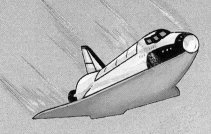

The astronauts open the doors of the cargo bay once the Space Shuttle is in orbit. They launch a satellite.

The engines are fired to make the Space Shuttle leave orbit and return to Earth. The heat shield below the Shuttle glows red-hot as it reenters the Earth's **atmosphere**.

The Space Shuttle glides in to land and lets down its wheels for touchdown. A parachute brings it to a standstill.

Inside the Shuttle

The Shuttle pilot and copilot each have a set of instruments so that either of them can fly the Shuttle.

The crew's living quarters are below the **flight deck**. Behind the living quarters an **airlock** leads to the cargo bay and the Spacelab.

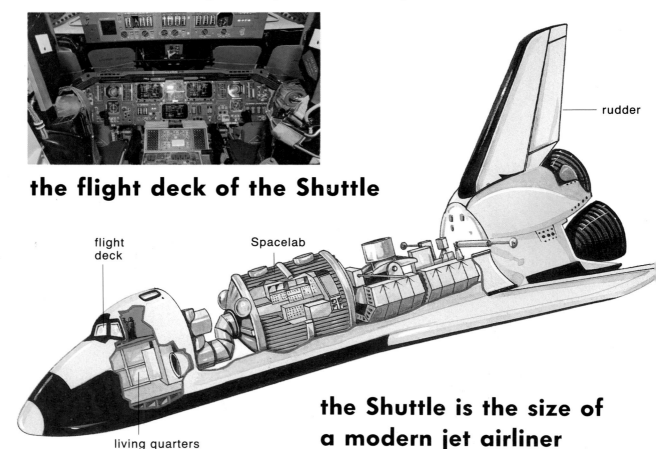

the flight deck of the Shuttle

flight deck

Spacelab

rudder

living quarters

the Shuttle is the size of a modern jet airliner

The cargo bay can carry two or three
satellites for launching into space.
It can also take small research projects
from schools and universities.

Our picture shows the cargo bay
with the doors open and boxes of
experiments in the foreground.

The Shuttle at Work

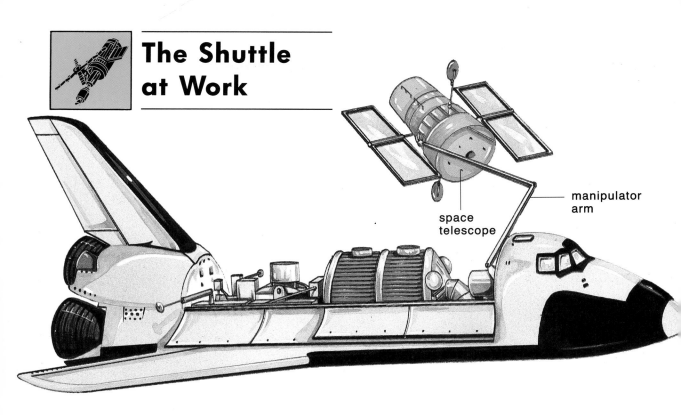

space telescope

manipulator arm

Besides the astronauts, the Shuttle transported scientists who carried out experiments. They did not need to enter the cargo bay. They could lift objects by **remote control**, using a **manipulator arm**.

Our picture shows Dr. Sally Ride, the first American woman in space, carrying out an experiment.

Spacelab

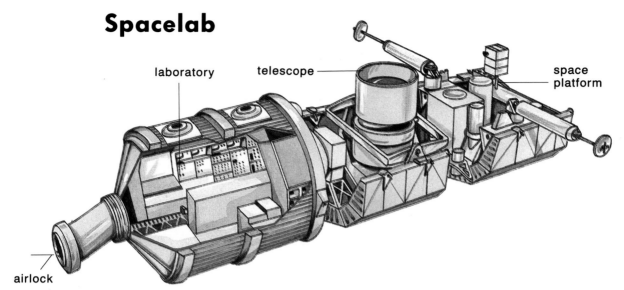

laboratory

telescope

space platform

airlock

In 1983 the Shuttle carried the European Spacelab fitted in its cargo bay. Spacelab was used by scientists to test metals and medicines in space.

The Shuttle may be used to launch a space telescope that will see farther into space than any telescope on Earth.

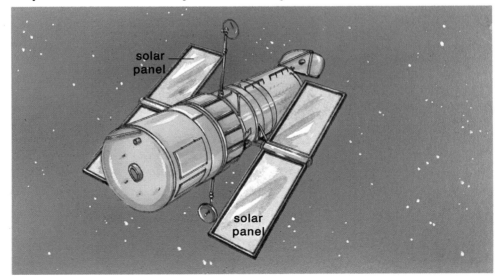

solar panel

solar panel

the space telescope

41

Future Space Stations

The next big step will be to put a space station into orbit around Earth. Spaceships will take crews to do special jobs and then take them back to Earth when their work is done.

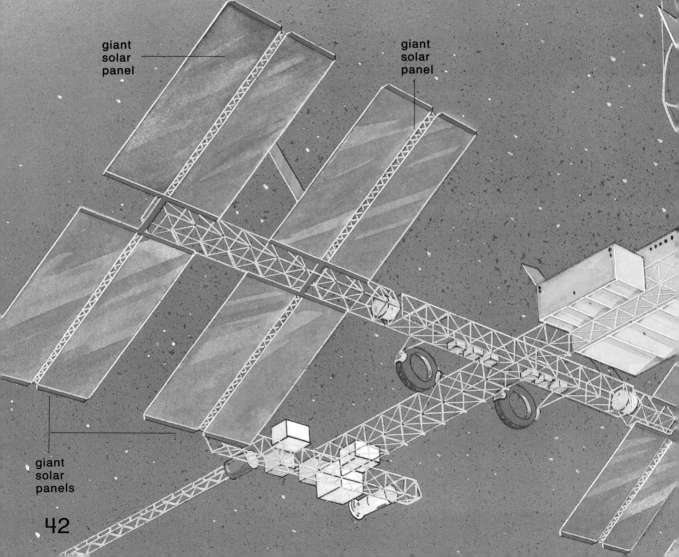

giant
solar
panel

giant
solar
panel

giant
solar
panels

A space station will have workshops to make things such as medicines and metals that cannot be made on Earth. It will have its own life-support system to supply fresh air and water.

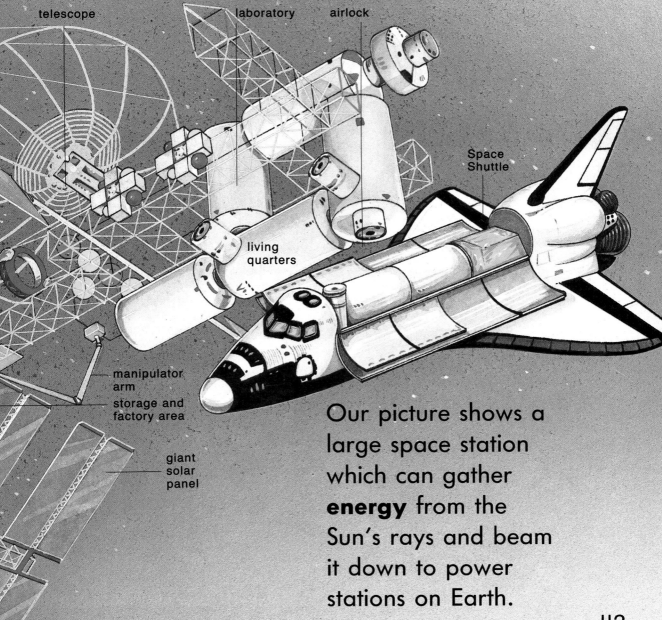

telescope

laboratory

airlock

Space Shuttle

living quarters

manipulator arm

storage and factory area

giant solar panel

Our picture shows a large space station which can gather **energy** from the Sun's rays and beam it down to power stations on Earth.

Colonies in Space

Fifty years ago no one believed that people would land on the Moon or travel through space.

It is very difficult to see what will happen in fifty years' time. The first stage might be to build a lunar base as shown in our picture. It may have a number of **inflatable** domes that could be used as homes and workshops.

Plants may be grown in huge plastic domes, and energy from the Sun would be collected by solar panels.

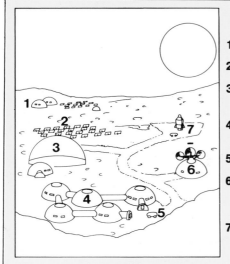

A Lunar Mining Colony of the Year 2025

1. Area where rare minerals are mined for use on Earth.
2. Solar panels for collecting energy from the Sun's rays.
3. Lunar garden. Vegetables grow in chemical "soil" beneath a clear plastic dome.
4. Living quarters beneath inflatable domes for mineworkers, scientists, and astronauts.
5. Lunar vehicle for carrying goods and people.
6. Base headquarters and command center. From here, movements of spacecraft and lunar vehicles are controlled by radio. Base can also speak to Earth.
7. Landing area and launch pad for lunar modules.

Glossary

airlock   a sealed room with special doors. It allows people to enter or leave a spacecraft without the air inside leaking into space.

antennae   equipment for sending and receiving radio signals.

astronaut   a person who has been trained to go into space.

atmosphere   the layer of gases that surrounds a planet. The Earth's atmosphere is the air.

comet   a small icy body in the solar system. A comet sometimes has a long ''tail'' that we can see from Earth. The tail is made of dust and gases.

command module   the control center of a manned spacecraft.

countdown   the counting aloud of the number of seconds, down to zero, before a spacecraft is launched.

crater   a bowl-shaped hollow.

dock   to bring together in space two spacecraft or two parts of a spacecraft.

flight deck   the place where the controls are in an aircraft or spacecraft.

gravity   the invisible force that pulls things toward the Earth or other bodies. Gravity makes objects fall and gives them weight.

hatch   opening in the side or top of a spacecraft.

heat shield   a thick layer of special material on a spacecraft to protect it from heat.

inflatable   an object that can be made bigger by pumping gas or air into it. A balloon is an inflatable object.

jet   a fast stream usually of gas or liquid.

launch pad   the place where a spacecraft is blasted off.

life-support system   equipment that supplies the astronauts with air to breathe. It also supplies food and water that keeps them alive.

lift-off   the moment when the spacecraft leaves the launch pad.

manipulator arm   a kind of crane used for lifting and moving other objects in space. Its joints are something like those in a human arm.

manned   with people inside.

orbit   the path of one body, like a planet or satellite, around another body. The Earth moves in orbit around the Sun.

oxygen pack   a pack containing air to breathe, which is carried on the astronaut's chest.

parachute   an umbrella-like object used to slow something down when it is falling or going too fast.

probe   an unmanned spacecraft sent to look at something more closely.

radio signals   sound waves carrying pictures or messages sent through the atmosphere.

remote control   the control of something from a distance.

robot   a machine that can perform tasks automatically without help from people.

rocket   a device used to launch a spacecraft. Its fuel burns and produces a jet of hot gases. The gases are sent out of the back of the rocket and push the rocket forward or upward.

rocket booster   additional rockets that help to give greater thrust to the main rocket engines at takeoff.

samples   small pieces of something, which show what the rest of it is like.

satellite   a small body in orbit around a large body. The Moon is the Earth's satellite. Human-made satellites circle the Earth. They are often used to send TV and radio signals.

solar energy   power that can be obtained from the Sun.

solar panel   a large flat area, or panel, that contains many solar cells. Each solar cell collects energy from the Sun's rays and turns it into electricity.

surface   the outside layer or top of something.

telescope   an instrument that makes it easier to see objects that are very far away.

thrust   the force that is used to drive a plane or spacecraft forward or upward.

unmanned   with no people inside.

weightlessness   a sensation of having no weight. An astronaut inside a spacecraft in orbit floats freely because there is no pull of gravity in space.

Index

Acknowledgments
The Publishers wish to thank NASA for their invaluable assistance in the preparation of this book.
Photographic credits (t=top b=bottom l=left r=right) Cover and title page photographs NASA/Science Photo Library; 9b ZEFA; 12, 13t, 13b, 15t, 17b, 20, 21b, NASA; 22 ZEFA; 23t NASA; 23b ZEFA; 26t, 26b, 27t, 27b, 30 NASA; 31t ZEFA; 31b NASA; 33t, 33b, 34t NASA; 38t ZEFA; 39, 40b NASA.
Illustrations by Paul Doherty, Keith Duran/Linden Artists, Steve Lings/Linden Artists, and BLA Publishing Limited.